DECAY NEVER CAME

David Kuhnlein

I0418257

MAXIMUS BOOKS
NORTH · FLORIDA
2023

ISBN: 979-8-9868347-3-3 (paperback)

Published by Maximus Books in the USA
First edition

cover: "Christ" by Odilon Redon
author photo by Kevin Killian
all collages by David Kuhnlein

for K

ACKNOWLEDGMENTS

Thank you to the editors of the magazines in which the following poems and collages first appeared:

Abandoned Library: 'December Dreams of Bukowski'
Alien Buddha Press: 'Nothing To Work On'
Annotations: 'Bloodborne'
BathHouse Blog: 'Sonnet to the Sea'
Expat Press: 'Decay Never Came'
Gutslut: 'Starfish'
Goats Milk Magazine: 'Gag' & 'The Tortured Still Alive'
Juked: 'Frank O'Hara in Thick Brown Socks'
Maximus: 'Sand Dollar' & 'Nautilus'
Misery Tourism: 'Knobbed Welk'
Prism Thread: 'Vision & Revision'
Rogue Agent: 'Wooden Spoon'

CONTENTS

I

dawn

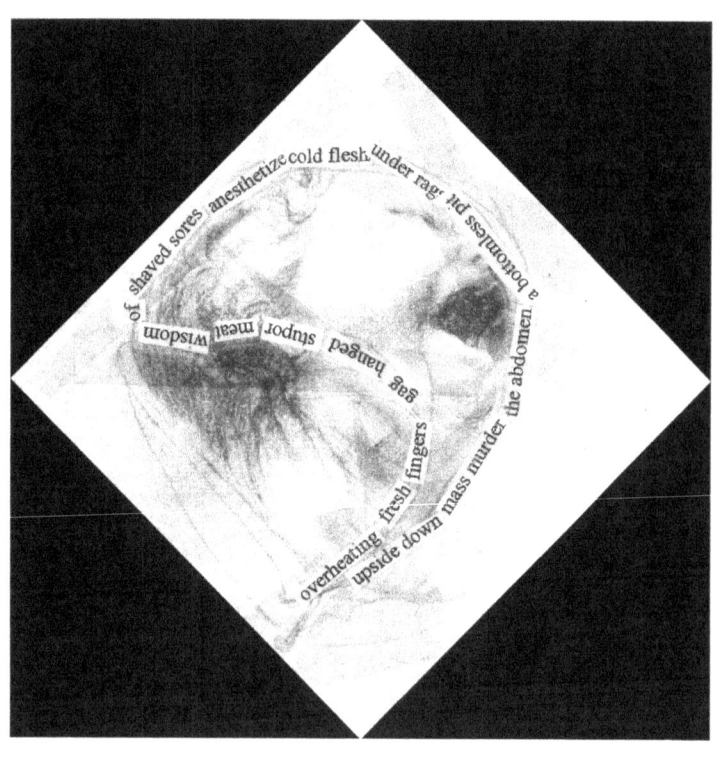

of shaved sores anesthetize cold flesh under rag pit a bottomless pit wisdom meal stupor meat hanged gag overheating fresh fingers upside down mass murder the abdomen

FRANK O'HARA IN THICK BROWN SOCKS

You say the mind is an idea
        the body has of itself
fizz
undecided between popping & not
                in my sparkling water
& I don't mind
                the way you
cling to the bottom of my glass
that never-ending hole becoming something
        more like ice in my hand

& even tho the way I look condenses
your skull when you hold me
over your bony shoulder I've seen the drip drop of dew
dangling from a fragile black cohosh shrub
its flowers heavy
w/ the insistence of your disease

grown in the shape
of arcane sigils
their roots held
somewhere just out of reach
like the
                earth

                id
                spirit
                genetics
are words
or minty candies in my mouth

there are a few things I'll never know about
the body because I am one you know
how it's impossible to see your own eyeball
               a decoration behind which one hides & plays
               adorning lingerie or a leather dog collar

a red leash w/ a gold chain & a red bow
          tightens around your neck
          as we swivel back & forth into the future
history a revolving door that feeds upon itself
                    & our sweat
          & so half-eaten & half-dressed
                    in the blue moonlight thru the window
                    we know to whom we belong

STARFISH

I'd paralyze the ocean waiting for a sign of life from you
Dumbfounded by that abyssal smile, floating sensitive to light
Our brittle infants spawn despite
The seawater I drowned my cells within
Five palms pressed in prayer, but my sins are unoriginal

I hooked you, mid-laugh, pissing on my asexual tube feet
Your granular arms dry gulping my vessel's hollow meat
Not even this musculature – a honeycomb of taste buds,
Water bugs, animal curves, deflated lungs –
Could soften the sphincter between our hug

My bag of blotted capillaries eversible inside my oral disk
I scarf your milk teeth, suction cup shoes, and pillowcase tongues
My weeping thirst carves a singular grave
For us in this ruin of beach sans melody
As the cackling sun crisps your tendons to mine, alphabetically

NOTHING TO WORK ON

The way your hands fumble for the coffee tin
In early morning, Larry lying curled between wool
Still warm from your body, his little tail wagging

Thermostat shrunken by the giant curve of moon
Through winter trees, I vanish in their darkened doorway
Before creeping back up beside you

Airplanes scrape the sky above the dog park
Their fog-trapped barks clipped short like grass
In a buzz cut, your hair mirrors freshly fallen snow

Sprouts of the lawn peek thru with sleepy eyes
The dog watches squirrels through a frosted pane
Drip coffee coughing, all of us, even the kitten, tremble

KNOBBED WELK

The welk crunched my memory in the loggerhead's neck. Torn paper thin through a jawbreaker. Trinidad bounced rubber on the loom. Shallow water denticles, rasping flesh, hulk the scar beneath my makeup. Skin flayed into the dream I knew I'd have once here.

Friendly sand, scraping my organism. I got a rash that doubled by breathing. A plate licked the mirror of my lower jaw. By the fire, horns were halved until made wax. I breed my objects by the knuckle. Clumping sparkled in the stump.

Bellies foamed, smiling rum. I don't feel anything above my stitches. Beefy men ate my wallet, proving to be crisp. Watching them suck milk from rocks, I buried my eggs within. Wet cement in my retainer.

Tooth-like marrow chalked the tongue, stratifying dunes. Chewing gum, dripping paint, a dextral specter sloughing air. Pestled down to a string that, when pulled, bites. Mud flats, sand flats, oyster hair.

Chowder's measured by the bugle. Sun schedules luncheons by the drum. The wrong gasses turned to stone. Inside the shell there was a map. But not enough of me to rot the warning.

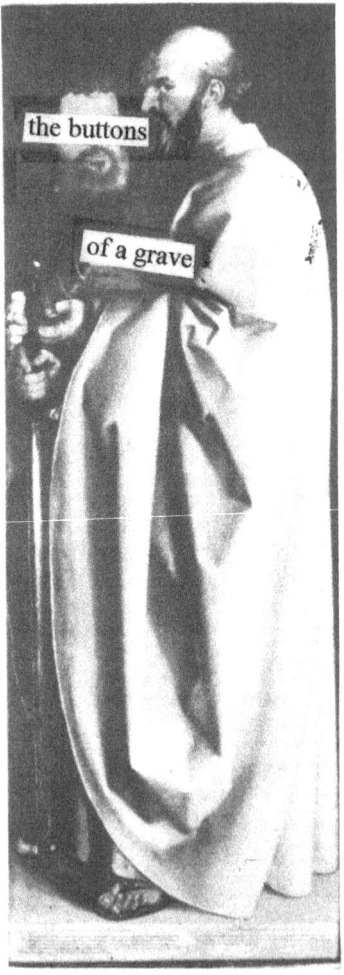

SAND DOLLAR

Time grins in ghost ridden creeks
Thumbing through my wave-shaped name
A benthic phantom, biscuit urchin
The mudflap of my pelvic floor

I grease the sky where birds struggle parting feathers
Parkways wade my residue, like carnassial teeth in drag
A funhouse mirror glosses my skeletal reflection
On crisp bleach bubbles I've swallowed

In untilled fields that crouch behind the sun
I smudge lipstick around holes
The ground zooms in till my kurgans are kissable
Deploying palmar, I hold the upper mud

Pacific townsfolk crave my cross-shaped uteri
Private joy remitted by my intercostal curves
Their mealy cores, horseshoed under
Fubsy tumors bolster bodies they destroy

Branches hiss at wind, like a god made good for entering
Riverbanks await edema, thickening felled trees
Stump's shape traced, buzzing with my blink
No stranger to the splinters in my gills reviving me

BIRD

In Memoriam Kevin Killian

the Matt Keegan gallery where each piece was a composite of two
side by side one on top of the other or shrunken down inside itself

each image a hairbrush or toilet seat becoming conscious
as if from their perspective they understood the bigger picture

as if there was a bigger picture Kevin said "think of Magritte
the man's face obscured by a bird you can't see anything at all"

from where I stood this attempted inarticulateness
or lack of symmetry by not attempting to render a face

even more beautiful when I imagined the point of view
of the man in the painting who never had eyes in the first place

noon

BLOODBORNE

Forbidden from my family home
Security cameras do nothing but flash me
Unscalable adobe dons a crown of broken glass
Greased and growing, thick as hair

My fingerprints dehisce their perimeter
Like psychotropics darting through blood
Red ants bite me in swells of cursive
Relatives' prayers teem, gleaning as they flay

I'm stuffed into a burlap sack
An unmarked truck, the station
They drill me more mouths to ball gag
And force feed me sneezes for lunch

I'm a dust cloud refusing to settle
Rot depressed back to life at its core
Fingered blue by a lineage drowned in me
Hallucinations abbreviated, gap to God shrunk

Reconstructing my jaw with a thicker lid
Is this a body bag or a river I'm in
The weak taxidermy of my surname thaws
Ashes melt up my knuckles without me

WOODEN SPOON

after Bob Flanagan's 'Bruises'

green stalks of lavender in
                          a field
       of it blooms purple on my thigh
I'd let you whack an entire history of
hot white stars

the galaxies in me! & isn't it funny
       how pleasure w/in pain
& not the other way around surrounds
me

       w/ pieces of the everyday

how I like you beneath me w/ yr neck
       craned in wanting
each hot white pulse in the sky
             turning purple night

I trace this constellation back to you
       in Westland clouded by the hum
of yr mother's oxygen machine
as my night

stand becomes an alter to you

wooden spoon wooden mala plastic
hairbrush (whack)
      who gets to decide
naughty or nice
      do we really want our coffee w/o
                    caffeine

or love w/o falling
      & instead of
orbiting like a yellow moon between us
      the way the night sky fills w/ clouds & light
                  from the city

sometimes nighttime like a displaced
bone
    no stars appear at all
that's when I'll ask where the pain has
gone
      that you've so graciously given me

until then I'll be here in this
half-dark
      staring at the changing phases
like the strange

                & lovely faces
         of that which you've impressed
upon me

     this little lonely bruise

SEAHORSE

The inside of your body
Remains unknown without violence
Once inside I can tell you
By your rings like a tree

The horses that I see in you
Pregnant with solitude
Your screened-in ligaments
In need of a broom

I pluck out your organs
Like fleas from thick wool
And your sawed open nostrils
Bubble back toward their hole

The space between hooves
Makes a bladder I squeeze
Every drop of the world out
Eyelids stapled to sleep

her
digestive open
grease lesions
stoned on braided
swelling in a
thighs cloud
formaldehyde

19

NAUTILUS

This is the edge of the Indo-Pacific
Where I watched the angel land
Her face so long and slender
Legs nestled the striated palm of my hand

This is my dream of connection
Reef reaching toward sky like a drawbridge
Fluting her feathers between
My eight-to-ten-headed appendage

This is her neck pulled under the water
As two arms I used for sailing shot
Above the waves and dragged her wails
Still echoing in my chamber pot

unless thou

arthroscopy

bind thee in

the splinter

comest quickly

there to remain

her eggs

oil pulling gasoline

cinnamon

in a glass vile

hooked aorta.

turning into

appearest in our circle with

enough shunts to debride god

stamped bodies

VISION & REVISION

When grandma cracked the blinds between us,
                    her eye etched me like a tombstone,
it was Plath I turned to in my mind: if not Plath, Muldoon.

Some poets fear the dead read their poems over shoulders,
                    zero distance, no revisions,
and she was: shadowed, disembodied,

bathroom window haunting, black hair
            floating, mist between the bristles
of her comb. Later that day would find me swimming

through her phantom perfume: Nina Ricci. The way
        ulnar bones made bracelets of her wrist,
pear-shaped smoke behind the window,

darkened the lung in segments, irreverent
        of this translucent thirst – eye milked over,
no heart beneath it beating, reading everything – I wrote.

SOUR MILK

after Rimbaud's 'Bad Blood'

Enchantment lies in the satyr's rug burnt knees, not the soup he stomps of my inner thigh. My words streaked red, rubbed out. Antennae to the ground, swigging through the snip, he ticks. I'm just a bloody igloo to this imp. Pink foam down my chin is emission enough. No wonder he's come to emaciate my accidents.

His teeth peel my thigh like potatoes, out of which pop rainbows of lead. My organs dribble like curd. In this milky period, I'm surrounded from the inside by crab shaped peptides. Reflected in his pupil, my amethyst eyes turn to stone. Pissed I poisoned his ecology, he dreams I varnish his every memory, without even impressing the stains. He makes snacks of my limbs with an ax; each crunch a resounding cum rag.

I praise his delicacy in securing my noose, tucking me undertow. I dangle beneath him, an aubade for his ass, from this translucent floor of hell. But he'll never escape the mess my insides made. I wiggle my trunk on its rope and look up as he unearths my dead mother. His hoof tacks her to the floor. I grow horns to meet them, to open her belly, and we take turns sipping cacodemonic slurs, bulked into my afterbirth.

dusk

DECAY NEVER CAME

There's a rotten socket inside my hull the hours never break
Listen as every cell pressurizes
Fluffed kernel of a torso giving births
To the hole that holds such warmth I've tied my paws

Spittle cascades, split ends of stamen moaning
The forest bends around honking birds
Beasts alphabetizing their antlers
Like moons cut in the door

The chatter of trees shapes the vine
Beneath which I masticate my suit
Sinking all sails, the wind recognizes itself
Where evolution balls between us, I open my muzzle and make
    room for tears

Geese squirt green between their web
Root bumped balsam hovers coloring, one only our cones can yolk
The globe's fat, a ward of tiny piazzas
A pyramidal welt behind the mask

I'm tallying sprees, rubbing strangers on all fours
Walls of skeet unzip

Cottage cheese purpling the day
Abortion scent, stained glass slept against, transparent beehives

Herniated before I was biology, in decay that never came
The neighborhood melts away justly to its sewage
I bark under a black matte paved green by droppings
Their texture knots in me

There's space to taste my mouth before it opens
Asphalt leashes pedestrians to an incisor's undertow
Wiggling them into milk
I exhume harder, like saliva that stays put

ghosts

fields of milkweed

sea salt

hibiscus

A Krishna devotee invites me to dinner. She cooks the tempeh extra bland, appealing to all my diseases. We perch on the corner of the table. The sounds of chewing, swallowing, and raising our voices mean something else. I fixate on bright yellow turmeric leaking from the potatoes to postpone my fantasies. Cold hands slip under her sari, lift the wire. My body, the giant strawberry I want her toes to stomp to juice. Seeds and fur balled red beneath her arches.

The dark, following Detroit's sunset, drapes us. The lotus carved in the back of her head feels like dune grass. Her lips are slugs that I've studied and still want to eat. A stick of incense burns us toward a room adorned with the prying eyes of a blue god who dances with milkmaids. Horns beneath my mat of hair don't prevent her from peeling back my sticky black tee-shirt. She licks the pentacle off my chest. Her tempo lulls me through devotion.

The floating island of our dream is strung with hundreds of miniature weights. What can be done to a nun to pluck those tendons? to cut the string? Mutual arthritis means our bones bend closer. It's uncanny, the pleasure that bubbles between us, like lubricant in a magic eight ball.

DECEMBER DREAMS OF BUKOWSKI

after Li Po

high in a castle, dilapidated
   gothic, bricks & stuff too small to name
fall away, plunk into the swamp below
   the water level rising

high on the sound of yr voice
   crumbling beneath yr feet, angelic
barely touch the ground, crumble
   crumble, like the chimney

you tell me yr dream on the phone
   mouthpiece opens to my eye like a keyhole
yr voice takes shape, a ghostly thing
   tending to Bukowski

the dilapidated, dying body of yr father
   IV overflowing w/ beer foam
   scraping the head w/ the back of yr hand
the water level rising

who's the damsel in this crumbling castle
   if I want to watch you nurse this poet

this part of yrself, back to health
    before bricks & things too sick to speak

emerge in the absence of his voice
    but I understand his poem by the way
yr waistline bows & hugs the side of his bed
    our tears too subtle to feel like tributaries run

back to health, back to yr dream building
    too haunted to appear, heavier than a brick
they fall, light rain thru cracks in the ceiling
    yr feet, angelic, barely touch the ground

    back into the swamp
the water level rising

SUNDIAL

You are a shadow eroded by rock
A dancing precursor to dentures
What are recompenses of life expectancy
When we're bespeckled paperweights at best

Boxing grit from sand for dinner
I churn the seafloor and look better when hanged
The barnacled architecture of my soft interior
This noose of veiny colors, brackish enough to gag home

You can't trapdoor me from loading my outerwear
With pastry dough, and charges of powder
Say the word, you know the word
And I become husks on behalf of your head

SOFT DISTANCE

after Wong May

to be felt amongst the soft distance of your hum
is rain in my neighbor's gutter draining slowly
there are lines like pointy shadows
gathering us in their elbow crutch
a neck hanging onto my head by a thread
how can one moment create so much noise
& the next & the next...

it's not the point to capture or even to ride alongside & observe
although I have my secret wants & treasure chests
buried in childhood notes
kept safe by memory's lopsided haggle
like a stupid dog half-asleep beneath the bed
a black paw recedes into shadow
& every eye, for a split-second, closes

the pain is gone, there is no pain
I've heard your cry in plastic water bottles
washed up & banging in the tide against my bedroom door
half-open & half-closed like my heart

SONNET TO THE SEA

He wants to know
What words are for
& I speak
Them awfully

Slowly
So his

Dreams might remain
Afloat like the alphabet
Grown into the shape of amoebas
Forgive me

My tongue too much resembles
The underside
Beneath your tender
Belly

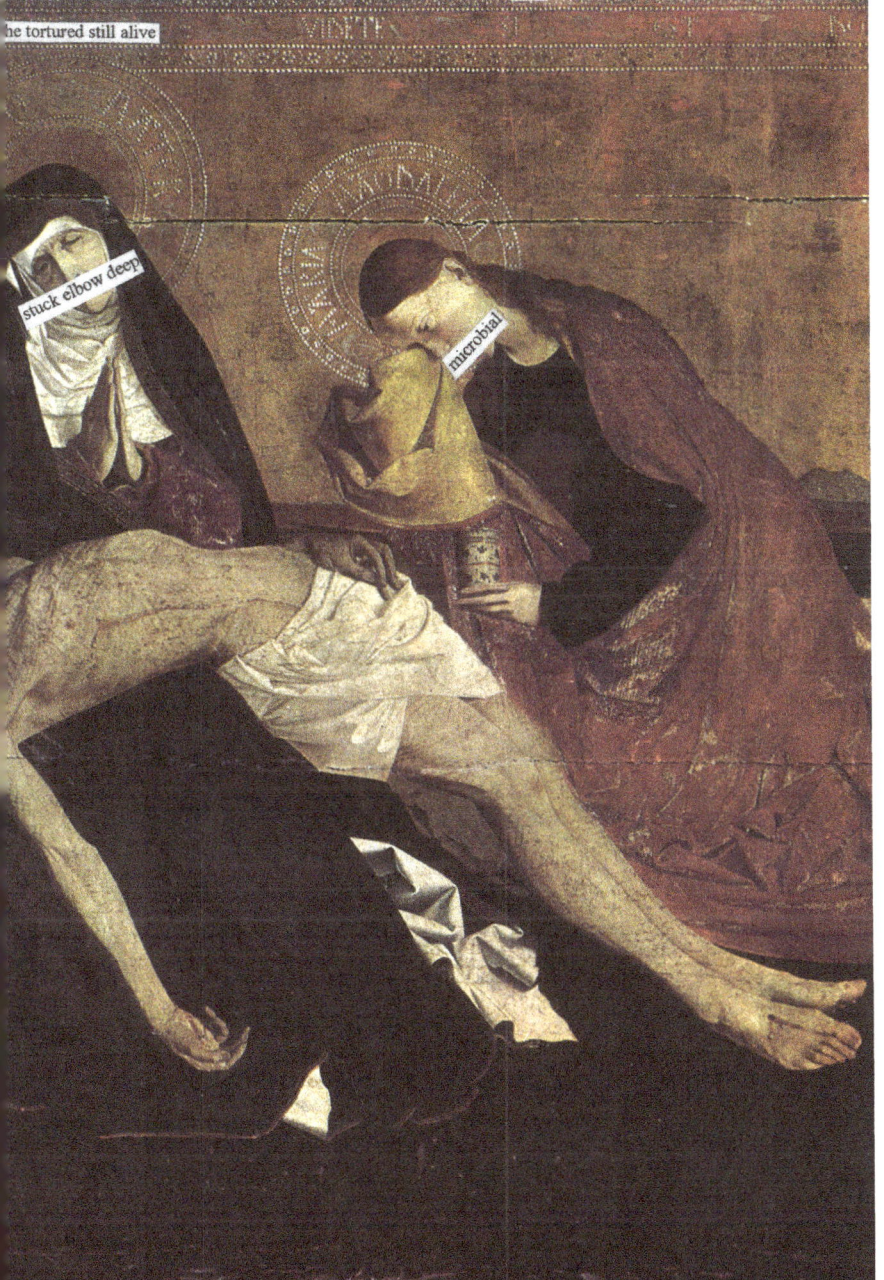

ABOUT THE AUTHOR

David Kuhnlein writes poetry, fiction, and criticism. His horror film reviews are collected in the zine Six Six Six, and his SF / Horror novella *Die Closer To Me* is forthcoming. He edits the literary review column *Torment*, venerating pain and illness, at The Quarterless Review. He lives in Michigan and is online @princessblood.